RESTORING ME JOURNAL

Girl get up!

O'MIA TYLET

Girl Get Up : Restoring Me Journal

ISBN: *978-1-964061-42-9*
Cover and Interior design by: *Nabin Karna*

S.H.E. PUBLISHING, LLC

Published by *SHE Publishing LLC*
Indianapolis, Indiana
www.shepublishingllc.com
info@shepublishingllc.com
Printed in the United States of America
First Edition: December 2025

Healing & Action

 ## DAILY PRACTICE

POSITIVE AFFIRMATION

"I give myself permission to heal at my own pace"

ACTION STEPS

List 3 things you will be more intentional about

_____

_____

_____

What went well today

_____

_____

_____

GRATITUDE

List 3 things you are grateful for today

1 _____

2 _____

3 _____

Where can I improve

_____

_____

_____

SELF-CARE

Self-care act for today

_____

_____

_____

Keep it or Burn it

Write freely. Keep what motivates you.
Tare and burn what you are ready to release

Trusting God - John 7:38; *Whoever believed in Me, as Scripture has said, rivers of living water will flow from within them.*

Keep it or Burn it

_____
_____
_____
_____
_____
_____
_____
_____
_____
_____
_____
_____
_____
_____
_____
_____
_____
_____
_____

LATE NIGHT REFLECTION

Today I learned _____

_____

_____

and now I feel like ☺ 😛 ☹

Healing & Action

 ## DAILY PRACTICE

POSITIVE AFFIRMATION

"My heart is learning to trust peace again"

ACTION STEPS

Speak one empowering affirmation out loud

_____

_____

_____

GRATITUDE

List 3 things you are grateful for today

1 _____

2 _____

3 _____

What went well today

_____

_____

_____

Where can I improve

_____

_____

_____

SELF-CARE

Self-care act for today

_____

_____

_____

Keep it or Burn it

Write freely. Keep what motivates you.
Tare and burn what you are ready to release

Self-Doubt - Proverbs 14:1; *the wise woman builds her house, but with her own hands the foolish one tears her down.*

Keep it or Burn it

_____

_____

_____

_____

_____

_____

_____

_____

_____

_____

_____

_____

_____

_____

_____

_____

_____

_____

_____

_____

_____

LATE NIGHT REFLECTION

Today I learned _____

_____

_____

and now I feel like   🙂   😛   ☹️

Healing & Action

 ## DAILY PRACTICE

POSITIVE AFFIRMATION

"I release what no longer serves my growth"

ACTION STEPS

Hydrate with intention

_____

_____

_____

What went well today

_____

_____

_____

GRATITUDE

List 3 things you are grateful for today

1 _____

2 _____

3 _____

Where can I improve

_____

_____

_____

SELF-CARE

Self-care act for today

_____

_____

_____

Keep it or Burn it

Write freely. Keep what motivates you.
Tare and burn what you are ready to release

Strength - Isaiah 41:10; *Do not fear, for I am with you; do not be dismayed, for I am your God. I will strengthen you and help you; I will uphold you with My righteous right hand.*

Keep it or Burn it

_____

_____

_____

_____

_____

_____

_____

_____

_____

_____

_____

_____

_____

_____

_____

_____

_____

_____

_____

_____

_____

LATE NIGHT REFLECTION

Today I learned _____

_____

_____

and now I feel like   :)   :D   :(

Healing & Action

 ## DAILY PRACTICE

POSITIVE AFFIRMATION

"I am worthy of rest, love and renewal"

ACTION STEPS

Take a mindful walk

_____

_____

_____

What went well today

_____

_____

_____

GRATITUDE

List 3 things you are grateful for today

1 _____

2 _____

3 _____

Where can I improve

_____

_____

_____

SELF-CARE

Self-care act for today

_____

_____

_____

Keep it or Burn it

Write freely. Keep what motivates you.
Tare and burn what you are ready to release

Purpose - Romans 11:29; *For God's gifts and His call are irrevocable.*

Keep it or Burn it

_____
_____
_____
_____
_____
_____
_____
_____
_____
_____
_____
_____
_____
_____
_____
_____
_____
_____
_____
_____
_____

LATE NIGHT REFLECTION

Today I learned _____

_____

_____

and now I feel like 🙂 😛 ☹️

Healing & Action

☀️ DAILY PRACTICE

POSITIVE AFFIRMATION

"Each breath I take brings calmness to my body"

ACTION STEPS

Declutter one space

_____

_____

What went well today

_____

_____

_____

GRATITUDE

List 3 things you are grateful for today

1. _____

2. _____

3. _____

Where can I improve

_____

_____

_____

SELF-CARE

Self-care act for today

_____

_____

_____

Keep it or Burn it

Write freely. Keep what motivates you.
Tare and burn what you are ready to release

Purpose - Romans 8:30; *And those He predestined, He also called; those He called, He also justified; those he justified, He also glorified.*

Keep it or Burn it

_____

_____

_____

_____

_____

_____

_____

_____

_____

_____

_____

_____

_____

_____

_____

_____

_____

_____

_____

_____

_____

_____

LATE NIGHT REFLECTION

Today I learned _____

_____

_____

and now I feel like 🙂   😛   🙁

Healing & Action

 ## DAILY PRACTICE

POSITIVE AFFIRMATION

"I honor my scars, they are proof of my strength"

ACTION STEPS

Write freely for 10 minutes

_____

_____

_____

What went well today

_____

_____

_____

GRATITUDE

List 3 things you are grateful for today

1 _____

2 _____

3 _____

Where can I improve

_____

_____

_____

SELF-CARE

Self-care act for today

_____

_____

_____

Keep it or Burn it

Write freely. Keep what motivates you.
Tare and burn what you are ready to release

Purpose - Ephesians 1:18; *I pray that the eyes of your heart may be enlightened in order that you may know the hope to which He has called you.*

Keep it or Burn it

_____

_____

_____

_____

_____

_____

_____

_____

_____

_____

_____

_____

_____

_____

_____

_____

_____

_____

_____

_____

_____

_____

_____

LATE NIGHT REFLECTION

Today I learned _____

_____

_____

and now I feel like 🙂 😛 🙁

Healing & Action

 ## DAILY PRACTICE

POSITIVE AFFIRMATION

"Healing is not linear, and that's ok"

ACTION STEPS

List your current emotions

_____

_____

_____

What went well today

_____

_____

_____

GRATITUDE

List 3 things you are grateful for today

1 _____

2 _____

3 _____

Where can I improve

_____

_____

_____

SELF-CARE

Self-care act for today

_____

_____

_____

Keep it or Burn it

Write freely. Keep what motivates you.
Tare and burn what you are ready to release

Trusting God - Ephesians 2:10; *For we are Christ's workmanship created in Christ Jesus, to do good works, which he prepared in advance for us to do.*

Keep it or Burn it

_____

_____

_____

_____

_____

_____

_____

_____

_____

_____

_____

_____

_____

_____

_____

_____

_____

_____

_____

_____

_____

LATE NIGHT REFLECTION

Today I learned _____

_____

_____

and now I feel like   🙂   😛   🙁

Healing & Action

 ## DAILY PRACTICE

POSITIVE AFFIRMATION

"I forgave myself for what I didn't know before I knew better"

ACTION STEPS

Forgive yourself for something small

_____

_____

_____

GRATITUDE

List 3 things you are grateful for today

1 _____

2 _____

3 _____

What went well today

_____

_____

_____

Where can I improve

_____

_____

_____

SELF-CARE

Self-care act for today

_____

_____

_____

Keep it or Burn it

Write freely. Keep what motivates you.
Tare and burn what you are ready to release

Trusting God - Romans 8:28; *And we know that for those who love God all things work together for good, for those who are called according to his purpose.*

Keep it or Burn it

_____

_____

_____

_____

_____

_____

_____

_____

_____

_____

_____

_____

_____

_____

_____

_____

_____

_____

_____

_____

_____

LATE NIGHT REFLECTION

Today I learned _____

_____

_____

and now I feel like 🙂 😛 🙁

Healing & Action

 ## DAILY PRACTICE

POSITIVE AFFIRMATION

"I am safe in this moment"

ACTION STEPS

Say NO kindly (protect your peace by setting boundaries)

_____

_____

_____

What went well today

_____

_____

_____

GRATITUDE

List 3 things you are grateful for today

1 _____

2 _____

3 _____

Where can I improve

_____

_____

_____

SELF-CARE

Self-care act for today

_____

_____

_____

Keep it or Burn it

Write freely. Keep what motivates you.
Tare and burn what you are ready to release

Trusting God - 1st John 5:14; *This is the confidence we have in approaching God; that if we ask anything according to His will, He hears us.*

Keep it or Burn it

_____

_____

_____

_____

_____

_____

_____

_____

_____

_____

_____

_____

_____

_____

_____

_____

_____

_____

_____

_____

_____

LATE NIGHT REFLECTION

Today I learned _____

_____

_____

and now I feel like   🙂   😛   🙁

Healing & Action

 ## DAILY PRACTICE

POSITIVE AFFIRMATION

"My body, mind and soul is aligned in restoration"

ACTION STEPS

> Light a candle for clarity (sit in silence for 3 min)

_____

_____

_____

What went well today

_____

_____

_____

GRATITUDE

> List 3 things you are grateful for today

1 _____

2 _____

3 _____

Where can I improve

_____

_____

_____

SELF-CARE

> Self-care act for today

_____

_____

_____

Keep it or Burn it

Write freely. Keep what motivates you.
Tare and burn what you are ready to release

Secret Things - Daniel 2:28; *There is a God in heaven who reveals mysteries.*

Keep it or Burn it

_____

_____

_____

_____

_____

_____

_____

_____

_____

_____

_____

_____

_____

_____

_____

_____

_____

_____

_____

_____

_____

_____

LATE NIGHT REFLECTION

Today I learned _____

_____

_____

and now I feel like   🙂   😛   ☹️

Healing & Action

 ## DAILY PRACTICE

POSITIVE AFFIRMATION

"I choose compassion over criticism"

ACTION STEPS

Spend time with Nature (get some sunlight)

_____

_____

_____

GRATITUDE

List 3 things you are grateful for today

1. _____

2. _____

3. _____

What went well today

_____

_____

_____

Where can I improve

_____

_____

_____

SELF-CARE

Self-care act for today

_____

_____

_____

Keep it or Burn it

Write freely. Keep what motivates you.
Tare and burn what you are ready to release

Trusting God - Thessalonians 5:24; *He who calls you is faithful; he will surely do it.*

Keep it or Burn it

_____
_____
_____
_____
_____
_____
_____
_____
_____
_____
_____
_____
_____
_____
_____
_____
_____
_____
_____
_____
_____
_____

LATE NIGHT REFLECTION

Today I learned _____

_____

_____

and now I feel like   🙂   😛   ☹️

Healing & Action

 ## DAILY PRACTICE

POSITIVE AFFIRMATION

"I deserve to feel whole again"

ACTION STEPS

Write a letter you'll never send (burn it if you like)

_____
_____
_____

GRATITUDE

List 3 things you are grateful for today

1 _____
2 _____
3 _____

What went well today

_____
_____
_____

Where can I improve

_____
_____
_____

SELF-CARE

Self-care act for today

_____
_____
_____

Keep it or Burn it

Write freely. Keep what motivates you.
Tare and burn what you are ready to release

Blessing - Psalm 51:17; *Walking in Obedience*.

Keep it or Burn it

Today I learned _____

_____

_____

and now I feel like   😊   😛   ☹️

Healing & Action

   M T W T F S

 ## DAILY PRACTICE

POSITIVE AFFIRMATION

"I let go of pain and made space for peace"

ACTION STEPS

Do one thing that makes you smile

_____

_____

_____

GRATITUDE

List 3 things you are grateful for today

1 _____

2 _____

3 _____

What went well today

_____

_____

_____

Where can I improve

_____

_____

_____

SELF-CARE

Self-care act for today

_____

_____

_____

Keep it or Burn it

Write freely. Keep what motivates you.
Tare and burn what you are ready to release

Obedience - 1st Samuel 15:21-22; *Waking in God's Footsteps*.

Keep it or Burn it

_____

_____

_____

_____

_____

_____

_____

_____

_____

_____

_____

_____

_____

_____

_____

_____

_____

_____

_____

_____

_____

_____

LATE NIGHT REFLECTION

Today I learned _____

_____

_____

and now I feel like   🙂   😛   🙁

Healing & Action

 ## DAILY PRACTICE

POSITIVE AFFIRMATION

"I am proud of how far I have come in my healing journey"

ACTION STEPS

Reflect on a past lesson then ask yourself what did it teach you

_____

_____

_____

GRATITUDE

List 3 things you are grateful for today

1 _____

2 _____

3 _____

What went well today

_____

_____

_____

Where can I improve

_____

_____

_____

SELF-CARE

Self-care act for today

_____

_____

_____

Keep it or Burn it

Write freely. Keep what motivates you.
Tare and burn what you are ready to release

Blessings - Luke 1:45; *Blessed is she who believed that what the Lord has promised will be fulfilled.*

Keep it or Burn it

_____

_____

_____

_____

_____

_____

_____

_____

_____

_____

_____

_____

_____

_____

_____

_____

_____

_____

_____

_____

_____

LATE NIGHT REFLECTION

Today I learned _____

_____

_____

and now I feel like   🙂   😛   🙁

Healing & Action

 ## DAILY PRACTICE

POSITIVE AFFIRMATION

"I allow joy to enter spaces once filled with hurt"

ACTION STEPS

Speak kindly to yourself all day

_____

_____

_____

GRATITUDE

List 3 things you are grateful for today

1 _____

2 _____

3 _____

What went well today

_____

_____

_____

Where can I improve

_____

_____

_____

SELF-CARE

Self-care act for today

_____

_____

_____

Keep it or Burn it

Write freely. Keep what motivates you.
Tare and burn what you are ready to release

Seeking God - Matthew 6:33; *But seek ye first the kingdom of God, and His righteousness, and all these things shall be added unto you.*

Keep it or Burn it

_____

_____

_____

_____

_____

_____

_____

_____

_____

_____

_____

_____

_____

_____

_____

_____

_____

_____

_____

_____

_____

LATE NIGHT REFLECTION

Today I learned _____

_____

_____

and now I feel like   🙂   😛   ☹️

Dear Future Self

I feel Safe

I am beautiful and I love the skin I'm in

I feel Joy

I am Grateful

I am Strong

I am exactly who God created me to be and I love Me

I am powerful

I am Kind

Dear Future Me

Write a letter to your future self

Healing & Action

 ## DAILY PRACTICE

POSITIVE AFFIRMATION

"My emotions are valid, and I honor them without judgement"

ACTION STEPS

Connect with someone who feels safe

_____

_____

_____

GRATITUDE

List 3 things you are grateful for today

1 _____

2 _____

3 _____

What went well today

_____

_____

_____

Where can I improve

_____

_____

_____

SELF-CARE

Self-care act for today

_____

_____

_____

Keep it or Burn it

Write freely. Keep what motivates you.
Tare and burn what you are ready to release

Prayer - John 6:37; *All those the Father gives Me will come to Me, and whoever comes to Me I will never drive away.*

Keep it or Burn it

_____

_____

_____

_____

_____

_____

_____

_____

_____

_____

_____

_____

_____

_____

_____

_____

_____

_____

_____

_____

_____

_____

_____

_____

LATE NIGHT REFLECTION

Today I learned _____

_____

_____

and now I feel like   🙂   😛   ☹️

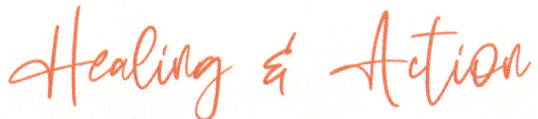 DATE : / /

 # DAILY PRACTICE

POSITIVE AFFIRMATION

"I replace fear with faith every day"

ACTION STEPS

Cook or eat a nourishing meal

_____
_____
_____

GRATITUDE

List 3 things you are grateful for today

1 _____
2 _____
3 _____

What went well today

_____
_____
_____

Where can I improve

_____
_____
_____

SELF-CARE

Self-care act for today

_____
_____
_____

Keep it or Burn it

Write freely. Keep what motivates you.
Tare and burn what you are ready to release

Peace - John 14:27; *Peace I leave with you; My peace I give you. I do not give to you as the world gives. Do not let your hearts be troubled and do not be afraid.*

Keep it or Burn it

_____

_____

_____

_____

_____

_____

_____

_____

_____

_____

_____

_____

_____

_____

_____

_____

_____

_____

_____

_____

_____

_____

_____

LATE NIGHT REFLECTION

Today I learned _____

_____

_____

and now I feel like   🙂   😛   🙁

Healing & Action

 ## DAILY PRACTICE

POSITIVE AFFIRMATION

"I am transforming my pain with power"

ACTION STEPS

Stretch or move for 10 min

_____

_____

_____

What went well today

_____

_____

_____

GRATITUDE

List 3 things you are grateful for today

1 _____

2 _____

3 _____

Where can I improve

_____

_____

_____

SELF-CARE

Self-care act for today

_____

_____

_____

Keep it or Burn it

Write freely. Keep what motivates you.
Tare and burn what you are ready to release

Grace - Matthew 11:28-30; *The Message*.

Keep it or Burn it

_____

_____

_____

_____

_____

_____

_____

_____

_____

_____

_____

_____

_____

_____

_____

_____

_____

_____

_____

_____

_____

_____

_____

LATE NIGHT REFLECTION

Today I learned _____

_____

_____

and now I feel like   🙂   😛   🙁

Healing & Action

 DAILY PRACTICE

POSITIVE AFFIRMATION

"The love I give myself is my medicine"

ACTION STEPS

Repeat a healing mantra

_____
_____
_____

GRATITUDE

List 3 things you are grateful for today

1. _____
2. _____
3. _____

What went well today

_____
_____
_____

Where can I improve

_____
_____
_____

SELF-CARE

Self-care act for today

_____
_____
_____

Keep it or Burn it

Write freely. Keep what motivates you.
Tare and burn what you are ready to release

Be Still - Psalm 62:1; *My soul finds rest in God alone; My salvation comes from Him.*

Keep it or Burn it

_____

_____

_____

_____

_____

_____

_____

_____

_____

_____

_____

_____

_____

_____

_____

_____

_____

_____

_____

_____

_____

LATE NIGHT REFLECTION

Today I learned _____

_____

_____

and now I feel like   🙂   😀   🙁

Healing & Action

 ## DAILY PRACTICE

POSITIVE AFFIRMATION

"I am learning to bloom again after the storm"

ACTION STEPS

Celebrate a small win

_____

_____

_____

GRATITUDE

List 3 things you are grateful for today

1 _____

2 _____

3 _____

What went well today

_____

_____

_____

Where can I improve

_____

_____

_____

SELF-CARE

Self-care act for today

_____

_____

_____

Keep it or Burn it

Write freely. Keep what motivates you.
Tare and burn what you are ready to release

Be Still - Philippians 4:6-7; *Be anxious for nothing, but in everything by prayer and supplication, with thanksgiving, let your request be known to God; and the peace of God, which surpasses all understanding, will guard your hearts and minds through Christ Jesus.*

Keep it or Burn it

_____

_____

_____

_____

_____

_____

_____

_____

_____

_____

_____

_____

_____

_____

_____

_____

_____

_____

_____

_____

_____

_____

_____

LATE NIGHT REFLECTION

Today I learned _____

_____

_____

and now I feel like   🙂   😛   🙁

Healing & Action

 ## DAILY PRACTICE

POSITIVE AFFIRMATION

"My inner peace is my priority"

ACTION STEPS

Do something creative

_____

_____

_____

GRATITUDE

List 3 things you are grateful for today

1 _____

2 _____

3 _____

What went well today

_____

_____

_____

Where can I improve

_____

_____

_____

SELF-CARE

Self-care act for today

_____

_____

_____

Keep it or Burn it

Write freely. Keep what motivates you.
Tare and burn what you are ready to release

Be Still - John 8:29; *The one who sent Me is with Me; He has not left Me alone, for I always do what pleases him.*

Keep it or Burn it

LATE NIGHT REFLECTION

Today I learned _____

_____

_____

and now I feel like   🙂   😛   🙁

Healing & Action

 ## DAILY PRACTICE

POSITIVE AFFIRMATION

"I thank my past for its lessons and release its hold on me"

ACTION STEPS

Journal 1 thing you've overcome

_____

_____

_____

What went well today

_____

_____

_____

GRATITUDE

List 3 things you are grateful for today

1 _____

2 _____

3 _____

Where can I improve

_____

_____

_____

SELF-CARE

Self-care act for today

_____

_____

_____

Keep it or Burn it

Write freely. Keep what motivates you.
Tare and burn what you are ready to release

Be Still - Psalm 46:10; *Be still, and know that I an God; I will be exalted among the nations, I will be exalted in the earth.*

Keep it or Burn it

_____
_____
_____
_____
_____
_____
_____
_____
_____
_____
_____
_____
_____
_____
_____
_____
_____
_____
_____
_____
_____

LATE NIGHT REFLECTION

Today I learned _____

_____

_____

and now I feel like   🙂   😛   🙁

Healing & Action

 DAILY PRACTICE

POSITIVE AFFIRMATION

"I trust the timing of my healing"

ACTION STEPS

Practice deep breathing

_____

_____

_____

GRATITUDE

List 3 things you are grateful for today

1 _____

2 _____

3 _____

What went well today

_____

_____

_____

Where can I improve

_____

_____

_____

SELF-CARE

Self-care act for today

_____

_____

_____

Keep it or Burn it

Write freely. Keep what motivates you.
Tare and burn what you are ready to release

Trust God - Romans 12:3; *Be careful not to block
your blessings.*

Keep it or Burn it

LATE NIGHT REFLECTION

Today I learned _____

_____

and now I feel like 🙂 😛 ☹️

Healing & Action

 ## DAILY PRACTICE

POSITIVE AFFIRMATION

"I became softer without losing my strength"

ACTION STEPS

List 5 qualities you love about yourself

_____

_____

_____

GRATITUDE

List 3 things you are grateful for today

1 _____

2 _____

3 _____

What went well today

_____

_____

_____

Where can I improve

_____

_____

_____

SELF-CARE

Self-care act for today

_____

_____

_____

Keep it or Burn it

Write freely. Keep what motivates you.
Tare and burn what you are ready to release

Unforgiveness - Ephesians 4:32; *Be kind to one another, tender-hearted, forgiving each other, just as God in Christ also has forgiven you.*

Keep it or Burn it

Today I learned _____

_____

and now I feel like   🙂   😛   🙁

Healing & Action

 ## DAILY PRACTICE

POSITIVE AFFIRMATION

"My heart expands a little more with each sunrise"

ACTION STEPS

Read or listen to something uplifting

_____

_____

_____

GRATITUDE

List 3 things you are grateful for today

1 _____

2 _____

3 _____

What went well today

_____

_____

_____

Where can I improve

_____

_____

_____

SELF-CARE

Self-care act for today

_____

_____

_____

Keep it or Burn it

Write freely. Keep what motivates you.
Tare and burn what you are ready to release

People Pleasing - Galatians 1:10; *Am I now trying to win the approval of human beings, or of God? Or am I trying to please people? If I were still trying to please people, I would not be a servant of Christ.*

Keep it or Burn it

_____

_____

_____

_____

_____

_____

_____

_____

_____

_____

_____

_____

_____

_____

_____

_____

_____

_____

_____

_____

LATE NIGHT REFLECTION

Today I learned _____

_____

_____

and now I feel like   🙂   😛   🙁

Healing & Action

 ## DAILY PRACTICE

POSITIVE AFFIRMATION

"I am allowed to rest without guilt"

ACTION STEPS

Take a social media break (day, week, month)

_____

_____

_____

GRATITUDE

List 3 things you are grateful for today

1 _____

2 _____

3 _____

What went well today

_____

_____

_____

Where can I improve

_____

_____

_____

SELF-CARE

Self-care act for today

_____

_____

_____

Keep it or Burn it

Write freely. Keep what motivates you.
Tare and burn what you are ready to release

Distraction - Proverbs 4:25; *Look straight ahead and fix your eyes on what lies before you.*

Keep it or Burn it

_____
_____
_____
_____
_____
_____
_____
_____
_____
_____
_____
_____
_____
_____
_____
_____
_____
_____
_____
_____
_____

LATE NIGHT REFLECTION

Today I learned _____

_____

_____

and now I feel like   🙂   😛   🙁

Healing & Action

 ## DAILY PRACTICE

POSITIVE AFFIRMATION

"I choose forgiveness not for others but for my freedom"

ACTION STEPS

Practice gratitude at night (name 3 peaceful moments)

_____
_____
_____

GRATITUDE

List 3 things you are grateful for today

1 _____
2 _____
3 _____

What went well today

_____
_____
_____

Where can I improve

_____
_____
_____

SELF-CARE

Self-care act for today

_____
_____
_____

Keep it or Burn it

Write freely. Keep what motivates you.
Tare and burn what you are ready to release

Facts - John 6:9; *Here is a boy with five small
barley loaves and two small fish, but how far will
they go among so many?*

Keep it or Burn it

_____

_____

_____

_____

_____

_____

_____

_____

_____

_____

_____

_____

_____

_____

_____

_____

_____

_____

_____

_____

_____

LATE NIGHT REFLECTION

Today I learned _____

_____

_____

and now I feel like   🙂   😛   🙁

Healing & Action

 ## DAILY PRACTICE

POSITIVE AFFIRMATION

"Every step I take towards healing matters"

ACTION STEPS

Do one act of kindness

_____

_____

_____

GRATITUDE

List 3 things you are grateful for today

1 _____

2 _____

3 _____

What went well today

_____

_____

_____

Where can I improve

_____

_____

_____

SELF-CARE

Self-care act for today

_____

_____

_____

Keep it or Burn it

Write freely. Keep what motivates you.
Tare and burn what you are ready to release

Indecision - Ecclesiastes 11:4; *If you wait for perfect conditions, you will never get anything done.*

Keep it or Burn it

Today I learned _____

_____

_____

and now I feel like 🙂 😛 🙁

Healing & Action

☀️ DAILY PRACTICE

POSITIVE AFFIRMATION

"I am light even after all I have been through"

ACTION STEPS

Write a "Future Me" Letter

_____
_____
_____

What went well today

_____
_____
_____

GRATITUDE

List 3 things you are grateful for today

1 _____
2 _____
3 _____

Where can I improve

_____
_____
_____

🧘 SELF-CARE

Self-care act for today

_____
_____
_____

Keep it or Burn it

Write freely. Keep what motivates you.
Tare and burn what you are ready to release

Comparison - Romans 12:6; *Lets just go ahead and be what we were made to be, without enviously or pridefully comparing ourselves with each other, or trying to be something we are not.*

Keep it or Burn it

_____

_____

_____

_____

_____

_____

_____

_____

_____

_____

_____

_____

_____

_____

_____

_____

_____

_____

_____

_____

_____

_____

_____

LATE NIGHT REFLECTION

Today I learned _____

_____

_____

and now I feel like 🙂 😛 🙁

Healing & Action

 ## ☀ DAILY PRACTICE

POSITIVE AFFIRMATION

"I am healed, I am whole, and I am free"

ACTION STEPS

Reflect on your month of healing

_____
_____
_____

What went well today

_____
_____
_____

GRATITUDE

List 3 things you are grateful for today

1 _____
2 _____
3 _____

Where can I improve

_____
_____
_____

SELF-CARE

Self-care act for today

_____
_____
_____

Keep it or Burn it

Write freely. Keep what motivates you.
Tare and burn what you are ready to release

Isolation - Proverbs 27:17; *As iron sharpens iron,*
so one person sharpens another.

Keep it or Burn it

_____

_____

_____

_____

_____

_____

_____

_____

_____

_____

_____

_____

_____

_____

_____

_____

_____

_____

_____

_____

_____

_____

_____

LATE NIGHT REFLECTION

Today I learned _____

_____

_____

and now I feel like   🙂   😛   ☹️

www.ingramcontent.com/pod-product-compliance
Lightning Source LLC
Chambersburg PA
CBHW051339120626
46547CB00016B/2608